THE POLE-VAULTER

Other books by Irving Layton in print:

Love Where the Nights Are Long (Editor, 1962)
Balls for a One-Armed Juggler (1963)
The Laughing Rooster (1964)
Periods of the Moon (1967)
The Shattered Plinths (1968)
The Whole Bloody Bird (1969)
Selected Poems (1969)
The Collected Poems of Irving Layton (1971)
Engagements: The Prose of Irving Layton (1972)
Lovers and Lesser Men (1973)

IRVING LAYTON
THE POLE-VAULTER

McClelland and Stewart Limited

© 1974 by Irving Layton

All rights reserved

Paper 0-7710-4863-7

The Canadian Publishers
McClelland and Stewart Limited
25 Hollinger Road, Toronto

Printed and bound in Canada

for
NADEZHDA MANDELSHTAM
and
HEDA KOVALY

> In the end it must be as it is and always has been: great things remain for the great, abysses for the profound, nuances and shudders for the refined, and, in brief, all that is rare for the rare.
>
> — *Nietzsche*
>
> We must live so we can tell what man is capable of doing to man. Perhaps this is God's will.
>
> — *Jew in Treblinka*

CONTENTS

Foreword/9
Departed/13
For Anne Frank/14
Midsummer's Dream in the Vienna Stadpark/15
The Final Solution/16
The Shadow/18
Mary/21
The Ventriloquist/22
Budapest/24
For the Fraulein from Hamburg/26
Bedbugs/27
Requiem for A.M. Klein/28
Lullaby/29
Lillian Roxon/30
September Woman/31
Corncrakes/32
Epigram for A.M. Klein/32
To the Woman with the Speaking Eyes/33
The Transfiguration/34
Religious Poet 1973 A.D./35
For Nadezhda Mandelshtam/36
Terrorists/37
For Andrei Amalrik/38
Poetry and the Class War/39
Leviathan/40
Harry Truman 1884-1972/41
Portrait of the Artist as a Young Bull/42
My Fair Lady from Bremen/43
Poet's Bust/44
Postcard/45
What I Told the Ghost of Harold Laski/46
Lines for My Grandchildren/48
Hit Parade/49
Thoughts of a Male Chauvinist Pig/50
The Solitary/51
The Animal Across the Street/52
Analogue/53
Honeymoon/54
For a Young Poet Who Hanged Himself/55
Lures/56

Funeraria 'Olea'/57
Mexican Guerrillas/57
Portrait of Someone I Know Too Well/58
A Tailor's View of History/59
Adam and Eve/60
Revolution/60
Marriage/61
Peacock/62
Some Other Day/63
The Black Queen/64
Mithymna Cemetery/65
The Basin/66
Molibos Cat/67
Afternoon of a Dying Satyr/68
Archilochus Curses the Woman Who Jilted Him/68
Madonna and Dionysos/69
The Ideal among Vacationists/70
Museum at Iraklion/71
Proteus and Nymph/72
American Young Woman in Patmos/73
Ganymede/74
Apokalypsis/75
Greek Fly/76
Poet on Cos/78
Greek Epigram/79
Madman/80
Jijimuge/81
Asian Suite/82
Conversion/84
Ravens/85
Ch'an Artist/86
Young Couple at the Lum Fong Hotel/87
Bodhidharma/88
The Three Sisters/89
Australian Bush/90
Encounter with a Reptile/91
The Coastal Mind/92
Pole-Vaulter/94
Acknowledgements/96

FOREWORD

This book began with my visit to the Anne Frank House in Amsterdam in July 1973, for much of it has been written under the shadow of her tragic death and the meanings it acquired for me in the weeks that followed. Despite the human wolves that were howling for her blood and that of her besieged family and their friends, all of them perilously hidden in an annex, she continued to write her imperishable diary and to avow her faith in human reason and goodness. Anne Frank, with her imagination and courage, is the prototype of all pole-vaulters.

The world is redeemed by its pole-vaulters.

Both National Socialism and Russian National Communism have aimed to degrade human beings to the condition of cringing slaves and robots. As the arrogant Nazis learned, just so the present masters of the Soviet Union are learning: the Jew with his tenacious faith in the creative principle and in human dignity is their unyielding antagonist. Surely it is no accident that the most prominent and the most spirited dissenters in that accursed land have been Jews: Pasternak, Daniel, Litvinov, Mandelshtam, Brodski, Ginzberg and the eminent physicist Sakharov, to select names almost at random. On the contrary, the fact of their dissent and fierce opposition lies imbedded in the logic of Jewish history itself.

The disaster that befell the vaunted Third Reich that was to endure for a thousand years is known to all. No less a disaster will one day overtake the communist empire that now stretches from the Pacific Ocean to East Germany. It is not I alone who foretell this; so does another favourite pole-vaulter of mine, Andrei Amalrik, serving a second term in Siberia on trumped-up charges for his truthful views on that foul and frozen turd which communists wish to hold up for mankind's reverencing, the U.S.S.R.

There are two books everyone living in the free world ought to read without delay. They are Nadezhda Mandelshtam's *Hope Against Hope* and Heda Kovaly's *The Victors and the Vanquished*. When he has finished reading them he will have a much clearer idea of what communism in practice means and of the part which Europe's spineless intellectuals played in fastening that hateful tyranny on the minds and backs of the regimented helots of Soviet Russia and its satellites. An authentic history detailing their grisly responsibility still remains to be written. Nadezhda Mandelshtam is the widow of Osip Mandelshtam, whom many consider to be the greatest Russian poet of the twentieth century. Along with hundreds of other gifted Jewish writers, he perished in Siberia on orders of Stalin, whose bid to be considered the most repulsive despot in history I believe to be unchallengeable. Heda Kovaly is a Czech Jewess who has written a movingly eloquent account of the stink and infamy that are National Socialism and Communism. She lived under their tyrannies and, magnificent pole-vaulter that she is, she survived them both.

It is with profound admiration and gratitude that I dedicate my book to these two extraordinary women.

However, it's not only in communist countries that a heartless materialism, fixated on power and possessions, has become the dominant outlook of our time. It is the metaphysics and theology of the free world as well, though here somewhat mitigated by competing traditions and philosophies. In my darker moments, when I reflect on the assaults being made on the integrity of the individual, on the frailty of his reason and sympathy, it seems to me the whole world is intent on turning out technical barbarians – people who can crank out perfect execution chambers coolly and expeditiously, as well as the emotionless technocrats to operate them at maximum efficiency. At such times I find the human stench intolerable and all poets become for me the ushers who used to spray incense into the aisles of the old Midway I used to go to every Saturday when I was a boy. Their triumph over the human reek, if I remember rightly, was illusory, at any rate short-lived.

Will the democratic nations also one day eliminate its thinkers and writers by consigning them to labour camps or loony bins? Will they too insist, as every communist country without exception does, that their citizens can only have approved official dreams; that it is an offense against the state not to be tolerated for anyone to have dreams of his own? For that is the crux of the matter and that is what poetry is all about. Poetry insists on the validity of each individual's dream, on his inviolable right to it, and on its import and value. There should be no mistake about this: the official approved dream is bad poetry. In dreams begin possibilities. At its best the official approved dream is bad poetry; at its worst it's a nightmare.

A marriage between technology and humanism is not an impossibility, certainly not. For the liberal democracies that is, and only if they remain alert and strong enough to withstand the assaults, external and internal, which Leninist totalitarianism must inevitably launch against them. Anyway, that is my hope, as it is of the polevaulters who have my love and admiration. To reflect, to doubt, to dream – if I can't do these things I don't want to live on this planet. You can wrap up the whole enterprise and stuff it up Brehznev's spacious fanny.

During my recent travels I picked up a Chinese saying: "Same bed, different dreams". The human condition with its satisfactions and inescapable miseries is the common bed of mankind but interpretations of it and of men's perplexity, torn as they are between being god and worm, differ from individual and individual, from nation to nation. The poet's task is to illuminate and clarify these dreams, firstly to the dreamer himself and afterwards to others whose dreams or cauchemars are shaped by a different culture or history. Even hideous dreams like fascism or bolshevism have to be interpreted through image and symbol so their inner reality can be understood and their hold on the sleepers who dream them broken.

In any event, that is how I see my vocation: to dream and to interpret dreams like my forbear Joseph and to spray from time to time the civet of poetry between the reeking aisles where people in civilized dress sit daydreaming of murder, violence and destruction, a smile of pleased gratification on their lips. Though I am often appalled by the joylessness and the illiteracy of the heart which I see spreading everywhere with frightening rapidity – if it continues it will kill off poetry just as surely as Macbeth murdered sleep – I shall continue to write poems for as long as inspiration lasts, though no longer, heaven or honesty forbid. For the good of my soul if for no one else's – and because I need the exercise.

Irving Layton
Toronto, Canada
May 7, 1974

DEPARTED

I walk the streets
of Amsterdam
            looking
everywhere for the faces
Rembrandt painted

The visages of burghers
unruffed & unruffled
(though a suspicion
in the clear light eyes
            the world's not always
ordered for the best)
arise to confront me

Unchanged
as the weatherstained gables
in their chartered banks
in their sleek pleasure boats

But where
are gone the grizzled ecstatic
faces
       of the vehement crazy men
who dreamed and prayed?

FOR ANNE FRANK

Clear-eyed sensitive Jewish girl
                               gay
with love of life the world
the strong-thighed and arrogant
never have wanted reasons
                        to seek
an end to us

Dear intrepid heart
dear chatterbox
you have given them
one more reason
—you and Jesus

II

Now many will live by your name

Because you are only a child
without medals and crucifixes,
a promise of goodness and talent
broken in half by the world's brutal hand

A tender lyric an equivocal destiny
forbade to grow into fertile splendour
and the anguish of unfulfillment
in the inconsolable tears of each of us

Anne, the abandoned of God
who yet sought and found Him
hiding behind your great terror:
who cloaked Him with your faith and love

A legend on your smiling lips
you move gently into the future
that greets you with the light
from your own sombre eyes and laughter.

MIDSUMMER'S DREAM IN THE VIENNA STADPARK

Auschwitz, as we know, is on the moon
And Belsen on Mars or Venus.
How can I not believe it?
The waltz strains are so entrancing

Anne Frank is alive and well
And so's her sister Margot;
In fact they're right here in the park
Seated beside the gentleman in the third row.

How handsome the two sisters look
—Anne's eyes, as always, are radiant;
They are drinking in the music
And can scarcely keep their feet from dancing.

And they praise the statue of Johann Strauss,
A single curve of pure delight;
Time sleeps on his violin
And he smiles at them all through the night.

Someone has gone to find their father;
He should be here any minute now.
Ah, happy man, run fast, faster.
Do not stop to wipe your brow.

For all in the park recognize Anne
And stand up as one to applaud her
Because though doomed herself she wept
When she saw gypsy children led to the gas chamber.

THE FINAL SOLUTION

It's been all cleared away, not a trace:
laughter keeps the ghosts in the cold ovens
and who can hear the whimpering of small children
or of beaten men and women, the hovering echoes,
when the nickelodeons play all day the latest Berliner
love ballads, not too loudly, just right?
Taste the blood in the perfect Rhenish wine
or smell the odour of fear when such lovely
well-scented frauleins are fiddling with the knobs
and smiling at the open-faced soldier in the corner?

History was having one of its fits—so what?
What does one do with a mad dog? One shoots it
finally and returns armless and bemedalled
to wife and children or goes to a Chaplin film
where in the accommodating dark the girlfriend
unzips your fly to warm her hands on your scrotum.
Heroes and villains, goodies and baddies, what
will you have to drink with your goulash? In art museums
together they're shown the mad beast wagging its tail
at a double-hooked nose that dissolves into ash

And appraised by gentlemen with clean fingernails
who admire a well-executed composition or pointed to
in hushed tones so that nothing of the novel frisson
be lost. Europe blew out its brains
for that frisson: gone forever are the poets and actors
the audacious comics that made Vienna and Warsaw
hold their sides with laughter. Gone, gone forever.
They will never return, these wild extravagant souls:
mediocrity stopped up their witty mouths,
envy salted the ground with their own sweet blood

Sealed up their light in the lightless halls of death.
Alas, the world cannot endure too much poetry:
a single cracked syllable—with a cognac—suffices.
I have seen the children of *reingemacht* Europe, their
queer incurious dead eyes and handsome blank faces,
leather straps and long matted hair their sole madness.
They have no need of wit or extravagance, they have
their knapsacks, their colourful all-purpose knapsacks.
The nickelodeon grinds on like fate, six fatties play cards:
the day is too ordinary for ghosts or griefs

THE SHADOW

I am a shadow. Everywhere, in the house
where I slip from my wife's embrace
as if her daily kiss turns me
inexplicably into vapour or a black cloud,
at the university where I teach teenagers
how to hide their emptiness and grow richer
than corn factors during a famine; even
my youngest son whom I love best
for he's my own childhood raised from
a cemetery of lies and guilts
cannot keep the awful metamorphosis
from happening or my uncontrollable
spastic feet from the trapdoor that sends me
swinging into space over the loneliest wolves

I release my shadow like a switchblade
or the cavernous grin of a ghost
as it spreads across the polished bannister
in failing traces that punctuate and pass,
even here in this well-lighted
Viennese hofbrau bursting with bodies
in clotted happy families of three or four
poised to reactivate bowel movements
through *brauten* and *schweinerfleisch,* to grease
with assorted dainties the secretions
of gland and skinpore; or playing cards
and drinking beer making a racket to awaken
Stahrenberg or that runt Dolfuss from the dead

I sit at my table, *nein* excuse me,
lie flat against the wall and manipulate
my filled glass like an aging acrobat
taking care not to spill a single drop
on their mothballed Nazi uniforms
or the undistinguished guttural faces
of the wives blanched by too much Catholic
piety—or is it pastry? Who wants to be
censorious at a moment like this, a moralist
when all are good-naturedly enjoying
the warm summery evening without a care,
stuffing their grudges against the world
a whole lifetime of self-hatred and resentment
into the tumblers they clink with friends
or in happy encircling arc with their neighbours?

Take me off the wall I shout from the wall,
don't leave me stretched out like some African skin
in a museum after the lights are extinguished
or like the silent spear in a corner absurd
and powerless menacing the ceiling;
teach me your indifference to great events
your boisterous pinkfaced affability as you slam
down your cards on the table as if they were fists
on an old Jew's skull, let me revel
in your ordinariness, in your guiltless murders
and the inescapable doom of your mediocrity
as you waltz down the Taborstrasse
with the Strausses, *vater and sohn,* directing
the orchestra with the baton of a clipped moustache

Teach me, O wretched modern clods
with lies and carnage in your genitalia,
how to love you, how to love every creature
on whom my shadow falls, humbled by the appalling
necessity that placed you here so that galaxies
may be explored and a divine few finally
defile through a ravine suspended only
by sunlight and music. Let me hug
you all to my breast, your mouths slavering
with goodwill and sincerity, my own no less
white and damp, I shout, but who hears my cries?
No one, no one. A tall man dressed for a fashionable
funeral at the Opera House rises invisibly
from one of the tables and gliding towards the door
scrapes off my shadow with his blue fingernails:
at dawn I grope my way to my child's hand

MARY

One of Abraham's chosen seed,
always I am stirred by pride and wonder
seeing Jesus and his Jewish mother, Mary,
reverenced everywhere so truly

Or coming on their imaginary likenesses
and that of Joseph, the world's adored cuckold
(it's rumoured a god performed his offices)
limned in paint or more enduring stone

In sunstruck squares or in old and greyskinned cathedrals
where men in special dress intone
incantatory rhymes to these beloved semites
begging of them favour and benediction

Always am I stirred, yet once standing
before an icon of the Virgin and her infant son
my heart broke for this ill-starred Hebrew woman
whose mute despair and tears were all for her martyred kin

THE VENTRILOQUIST

The brightly painted puppets
are in their places again:

Smiling to one another
over the butchered meat of cows and sheep
the spiced legs and wings of braised chicken
talking chortling crowing
blinking their eyes in affection
or good humour, cracking jokes
and giving each other sly digs
to put the table in an uproar of merriment

To add to the realism
the pink-faced waiters are perspiring
the manager wearing frown and black gaberdine
hurries towards the solitary diner
and the radio plays a Mendelssohn *lied*

In a far corner of the restaurant
two shadowy figures at set intervals
move the Gothic chess pieces across a board
as if they were miniature landmines

And at a given signal
the six card-players stop their game
to argue hotly the political news of the day:
the brutal killing of a party leader
of surprising astuteness
and manoeuvrability

Unexpectedly I overhear from another table
someone say I adore you Lisl, I love you Lisl
and a puppet in slacks and purple blouse
murmur sadly I love you too Heinrich

Though I look everywhere for him
the diabolical ventriloquist
is nowhere to be seen

Vienna,
July 1973

BUDAPEST

Doktor Marx
    old swarthy rabbin face
        ferule behind your back
            to crack knuckles with
Is this what you wanted?
    dilapidated run-down lives
        nosing out valuta and your famous
            Manifesto under a grubby deck of cards
Because the perfect revolution
    (yours) has been made
        and now there's nothing else
            to do with one's life?

Listen, you Prussian asshole
    the funky aristos
        hated equality
            more than the pox
But everything beautiful
    in this city
        was their idea
Though castles churches palaces gracious parks
    do look like amnesiacs
        trying to recall something
            in the pallid sunshine
And elegance is a feeble old woman
    selling flowers
        in the marketplace
A bygone irretrievable beauty
    IBUSZ and the proles exploit
        while posing as experts
            on the bowel movements of history

Which is alright with me, Herr Marx,
        as long as you and they
                let me know in good time
                      which way the wind's blowing
For my impartiality
        between whites and reds
                is you may believe me
                      nothing less than godlike

A poet's colours
        are green and black
                the colours of life and death
And his Internationale begins:
        let's all fart in the ears
                of commissars and priests
And I'm here
        in this faded city only
                because I hope to find
                      behind all these scurrying bones
                              one unfearing authentic man

IBUSZ *is the Hungarian Travel Agency*

FOR THE FRAULEIN FROM HAMBURG

Poor mortal
you show a white-coated tongue
to the world

Bone-weary of the political leaflet
hash
and the occasional excitation
of your clitoris

Even the misery
of other despoiled humans
superfluous like yourself
no longer cheers
or relieves the ache
of your cureless insignificance

You hold up fists
to be manacled, fraulein,
and shrewder decadents than you
will again congeal your nullity
into the slavemaster's whip

BEDBUGS

The thugs the red bedbugs
are hunting down Solzhenitsyn

They want his blood
they want to make him over
into the 'new man' (read 'corpse') Lenin
dreamed of for mankind before he croaked

Noble Sartre is mute
not knowing what to do with his dirty hands
and Simone de Beauvoir numb
from staring too long at her mildewing crotch

He has a bad chest cold
or Pablo Neruda would surely speak out loud and bold
and at once hand back all the medals & prizes
the Soviet poultry-lovers gave him

Who will volunteer to dig up
Auden and Spender from the thirties? Koestler?
Alas, only Orwell still speaks from the grave

There's no imperial voice to scare away the bedbugs
no sudden torchlight to make them scurry from panic

Intellectuals always have had a ripe talent
for servitude, an exquisite taste for it:
ask those magnificent pole-vaulters
by whom a guilty Europe is redeemed

—Nadezhda Mandelshtam and Heda Kovaly;
they will supply you with names and addresses
and tell you true horror stories
to sicken and purify you

Stories to keep you howling all your life

Molibos, Lesbos,
September 6, 1973

REQUIEM FOR A.M. KLEIN

I remember your cigarette-stained fingers
The rimless glasses that glinted with your wit
And the bowtie protruding
Under your chin like a spotted tongue

Your scholar's mind neat as your hair
And the jaunty self-loving complacencies
That made me think of plump pumpkin seeds
Falling from your mouth, the epigrams

I finally gave up counting
Scattering like the pigeons on St. Mark's square
When a piston ring suddenly explodes.
I still wonder at your psychological obtuseness

And the sentimentality each clever Jew
Misconstrues for sensitivity:
Fool's gold which you, O alchemist,
Changed into precious metal, solid and true

Warm-hearted egotist, my dear unforgettable Abe,
You were a medieval troubadour
Who somehow wandered into a lawyer's office
And could not find your way back again

Though the reverent adolescent
Like the Virgil which fee-less you taught him
Would have taken your hand and led you out
Muttering the learned hexameters like a charm

Now grey-haired I diet, quarrel with my son,
Watch a young girl make love to herself,
Occasionally speak to God and for your sake
Resolve to listen without irony to young poets

But still muse on your bronzed tits of Justice.
Yes, here where every island has its immortal bard
I think of you with grateful tears and affection
And give them your fresh imperishable name

LULLABY

Uncaring, the Danube runs on;
Blue or red, it does not want to know.
Molecules of water don't change
And whoever drinks it drinks H_2O.

Horthy's face is at the bottom
And moles and ash is Comrade Stalin;
The bright blood flows from blues and reds
And the fish die out and the worms crawl in.

LILLIAN ROXON

Asthmatic and always stuffing your face;
Your lymph glands brimming with chemicals to control
Unavailingly your adiposity and sinister wheezings;
The sudden breathlessness that threatened each time
To unhook your fat body from your soul. . . .

You've taken the whole works into the grave
With you. After all the noisy convulsive shakes
Like those of a resistless locomotive rumbling
Out of the station—silence. Uncanny silence.
Not a single wheeze can ever startle you awake.

Death, the fathead, struck you when you were alone;
Stabbed that great heart of yours, sparing
The mediocrities and prudent losers you scorned.
So many lumps to choose from, their numbers increasing,
And that dull jerk must come and strike you down.

My dear incomparable Lilli, I find it strange to think
I shall never hear again your indecorous wit
Or see your wide luminous eyes glitter with humour
And affection. Unencumbered, now lighter than air
My fat companionable pole-vaulter, you leave the ground and soar.

SEPTEMBER WOMAN

She unclasps her brassiere
and lets her breasts fall on his face
like ripe-heavy melons

He shuts his eyes
to imagine the many enraptured hands
that reached out for them.
the firm lips that once quivered with passion

He imagines her imagining him imagine this

The season's pathos envelopes them
like an echo
and makes them one with the lonely stubbled field

However sweetly she smiles
he is aware of the silver fillings in her teeth,
the disappointed tenderness in her fingers
when she touches him

Feeling on his bared skin
she is divided between desire
and the mockery of it
as she pushes her thick body under him

CORNCRAKES

Why do the corncrakes
wake me each joyous morning
with their cries
of 'Zazu Pitts' 'Zazu Pitts' 'Zazu Pitts'

I too found
her wistful flutterings
on the movie screen
funny
        and loved her
for the nameless ache
she brought
           like the sadness
of an open barndoor at dusk
or the hands of old people

But she's been dead
               for years
and no one remembers her anymore

EPIGRAM FOR A.M. KLEIN

They say you keep the devils laughing by your wit
And all the furnaces stilled that they may hear it.

TO THE WOMAN WITH THE SPEAKING EYES
For Rae Sampson

It is not men you fear
but the tenderness they make you feel for them

And your resentment is not against men
but against the unfair division of the universe
into pestle and mortar, mountain peaks and valleys

Dark your beautiful eyes and tragic:
they have seen too many fearsome transformations
of smooth pluckable mushrooms into clubs and truncheons

Your desirable breasts are a burden to you
and through your Caesarean cicatrice
is an arrow that points directly
to where all men and angels would wish to lie
your supple pleasure-promising legs are closed
against them like inhospitable Abrahams

Unsure of the planets that rule, finally
you walk away hand-in-hand with your pride
leaving behind your modern confusion
for philosophers to unravel

THE TRANSFIGURATION

On the beach I feel like a special spare part
or an important tool left lying on the stones
which someone will come soon to reclaim;
knees to chin I begin to suppose some god
has placed me here as a human question mark
for me to imagine but never to perceive;
I'm haunted by other such images that swarm
out of my self as bees from a cracked hive

All the long afternoon unthinkingly
people walk through my metaphors of them
or plunge into my perilous abstractions
as gaily as they plunge into the sea;
a woman, for instance, bites into her tomato
scattering the yellow seeds which fall
quite easily into poems not yet written
together with the salt grains on the tip of her lip

If I sit up to argue about Chilean politics
or about Nerval's poems I feel somebody else
has borrowed my mouth for ten minutes.
I say it's hopeless. I shall tie a heavy stone
to these anguished transcendental feelings of mine
and drop the lot into the smiling bay;
washed by the sea they will surface as white blossoms
which the tide will present to me on bent knees

RELIGIOUS POET 1973 A.D.

Like an all-night loser in despair
he puts his money on the fatal number
and goes for broke; and ends with that strange pair,
Jesus and cirrhosis of the liver.

His fawning penitence is half truth half bluff
for through the garbling haze of alcohol
he sees damnation summoned by the Fall
and guilt spasms routine as his cigarette cough

But who so punished him for his lousy sins
to reveal them in bad poems that read like bulletins?

FOR NADEZHDA MANDELSHTAM

Nadezhda, my grey-haired love, my wrinkled darling
I write you from the cold whiteness of Toronto
Hoping my affection for you thaws the ice and snow
Between us, melts the barbed wire around your heart.

Tough gallant lady, you're so much like my mother.
She too would have spat at the Kremlin's mountaineer,
At the contemptible pygmies and half-men who let him
Play tunes on their skulls with his grubby fingers.

I've friends with soft hearts and softer heads
Who grieve when fire rains down on evil men
And perhaps you also see the bulging eyes of the dead
And feel the stink and silence that surrounds them

As they move into history. Perhaps like them
You also march in groups, sign petitions, disapprove
Of America's might, saying what message has poetry
For this sad demented world except love.

Perhaps. But not I, my grey-haired darling.
When freedom flings his fiery horseshoes they explode,
Sending scorching nails with a loud noise
At the heads, eyes and groins of my enemies.

In a hard school it was drilled into me
To tumble vermin into a hot cauldron death;
In the dungheap of contemporary history
The Stalins hatch everywhere. The poet must break

Their backs with a hammer's blow.
One does not fool around with broad-chested Ossetes.
One does not wait to see their cockroach whiskers grow.
Were Osip with us he'd have my sad ache and agree.

TERRORISTS

Insulted, forsaken exiles
harried, harassed, shat on
learning
        Justice is heard only
when it speaks through the mouth
of a cannon

learning
        Right lies waiting
to fly out of a gun barrel

learning weakness is the one crime
history never pardons or condones

Uselessly you bruise yourselves, squirming
against civilization's whipping post;
Black September wolfcubs
terrify only themselves

The Jewish terrorists, ah:
Maimonides, Spinoza, Freud,
Marx

The whole world is still quaking

FOR ANDREI AMALRIK

Who speaks up for you, Andrei Amalrik?
Worse yet, today for whom do you speak?
Forsaken and more alone than any heretic
Who whitened into ash—where are your guns? Your bombs?
Brave soul, you have none. You have none.

Into the gas ovens with you like a helpless Jew
Into the slave camps or Kolymna mines
You have a mind; it is your ruin
Imagination and spirit; they are your undoing
Integrity. Luckless man, in these times? You are doomed.

Your ears were not fashioned for loudspeakers
Your eyes for the blueprints of beehive utopias
Your published wit as packing for Lenin's ravings
The experts east and west want to squeeze oil
From your pores to keep their factory cylinders purring.

Your martyrdom means nothing to the young
With close-cropped slogans between their ears
And their terrible blank faces. Nothing. In East Berlin
To the red refuse swept up from every land
A thing to sneer at and entomb in Siberian silence.

You are a bitter portent for mankind, Andrei
As ominous as the death of Anne Frank
Swiftly the sun sinks and shadows mount the hill
Who besides yourself cares about freedom?
Only the wolves you see from your barred window.

POETRY AND THE CLASS WAR

So long as there's injustice and the class war
Prepare for murder, baseness of every kind;
Man is damned and incurably ill his mind:
Finding reasons to slay is what he's made for.

In this they're one: rich, rotos, hoi polloi.
There is no obloquy that is beyond them;
Inventing novel horrors keeps them trim,
Torturing and maiming is their sweetest joy.

In vain, in vain, you write in praise of love:
Church-going and poems make the human smell
Less outrageous to each and less fearful.
Men stink in their own nostrils and yet approve.

A cultured man can see a woman torn
Or blind a child before his mother's eyes;
Morality is the choicest of his lies,
On his wolf's head he displays it like a crown.

Look for no mercy caught between rich and poor
But slave camp and firing squad and the gas oven.
He spoke for the age, Lenin lost in Beethoven:
'We must break skulls, alas—then break some more!'

Poets are ushers in the old Midway
Spraying a tender civet into the aisle;
On either side are civilized killers who smile
And whose reek no essence will ever oversway.

LEVIATHAN

Faith or ideals lacking
how will they resist
another tyrant or dictator?

Luckily
no one has the will or energy
to enslave them either:
they also are lacking

Only boredom
will ever conquer them again,
the futility
they find each night in their own
mirrors

Out of their effluvium
and collective nothingness
is built
the final Leviathan

HARRY TRUMAN 1884-1972

Left-hand of justice, great god of war,
Whose naked blade in a fateful hour
Engrafts virtue in men and nations:
Let mine be courage and occasion
To send, for mankind, death to humans
In their thousands—death long-drawn-out and
Vile or swift as the bleeding meteor
That scorches the night and's seen no more;
Or as sudden puffs of smoke that drift
Across desert wastes when the wind shifts.

History, a grand success story,
Impatient of groans that lack glory,
Is disregardful of the wronged slave
Howsoever handsome, tall and brave
But has an easy flattering smile
For his captors, callous and doomful.
So my deed, nourished in the womb of fate,
Washed of its birthstains, men will rank great;
And I neither feel nor seem evil
But die an old man, honoured by all.

PORTRAIT OF THE ARTIST AS A YOUNG BULL

Looking like an old bull suffering
from hemorrhoids the Minister
   of Health
warmly complimented the other
   bulls;
artists, he called them, *really*
   artists

And our very best, our *very* own

I thought of them pawing
the ground with their hockey sticks
and of the fine
melancholy face of Solzhenitsyn

MY FAIR LADY FROM BREMEN

Fraulein,
you have brave aristocratic eyes
and I like the way
you hold your small Viking head
and shake my hand
but why do your lips
when they're not smiling gaily
curl with such sour disdain?

Alas, you've no talent
for insight for self-awareness and irony
(Irony? What German ever had any?)
and the clever nervous Jews
who might have told you why your mouth
sometimes has the look of a cankered roseleaf
your countrymen gassed
and afterwards burned

The devil alone could tell
what you are running so briskly from,
what ghosts or hell,
but I have the notion, watching
your birdlike agitations
what you most want from the fates these days
is a hard phallus between your burnt legs
to loosen you up
and let you feel warm and human again

POET'S BUST

Firmly he held the sword in his hand:
he glared at the snakecurled head in the mirror
and lopped it off with one sweep;
his senses extra sharp to the end,
he heard it fall at his feet

Untangled are the pendant curls,
lordly now is the smile on his lips;
his face inscrutably serene
melts the conqueror's heart of stone:
young girls gaze at the scaleless eyes and dream

POSTCARD

For Aviva

In Venice
when it stormed
(ah, where have the years fled?)
you clasped me to you
in terror and love

Each thunderclap
was a fresh embrace
under the sheets;
we were never so close
as when the elements
seemed bent to destroy us

Tonight
as if another
War of Liberation
were in progress
thunderclashes
rock Budapest
and flares
light up the city
to direct fiery
salvos of rain
against roofs and bridges

Marauders
are hammering
on the windowpanes
and I cower
under my blanket
—but where are you, my love?

WHAT I TOLD THE GHOST OF HAROLD LASKI

There are days when I think of nothing
but politics:
wasted precious hours taken
from poem-making love-making and fine conversations
about fellatio in ancient Abyssinia
or collecting and watering beach pebbles
to surface their magnificent colours
from somewhere deep inside them;
I've seen them brighten with a luminosity
no one in his right mind or not forced to
would ever impute to the faces of Franco
Richard Nixon or old sourpuss himself, Kosygin,
his lower bowel constipated with bolshevism

Name me three statesmen
who ever wrote a line of memorable poetry
I don't mean rhetoric, I mean poetry
though Lincoln's melancholia comes sometimes close
and the passion of Fox and Demosthenes

But would you really quote Lester Pearson
to the girlfriend taking off her panties
and you wanted the clinching line
to make it hot and good?
Or Dief the Chief though that adman's tag
rhymes with grief
at the funeral of a young much-loved child?

After all poetry is as private as a sigh
though the whole world hear it;
politics, public and impersonal
as a civic lavatory or bus:
it's the trough
at which all push and shove
the rich bastards that have too much
and the poor bastards that don't have enough

One day when I'm not expecting it to happen
I shall look up and see the Parliament buildings
all going up in pamphlets and smoke,
and seeking out the Prime Minister
I'll find him under his desk
haranguing a visiting contingent of pygmies
on the grace and benefits of lowliness.

Out of gratitude for his eloquence
they ask me to present him with a toupee
made from their daughters' pubic hair
before I wrap myself in the Maple Leaf
and make myself completely invisible.
Instead, I hand him this poem
and tell him to use it as a visa
for heaven

Yes, there are days when I think of nothing
but politics
but they are not my best days

LINES FOR MY GRANDCHILDREN

there are only two kinds of people
masters and slaves
now and always the greater number
are slaves—to tradition marriage
family state or cause
they are cowards who ask to be manacled
and their minds put to rest
or who want to go to sleep
their noddings taken for wisdom and serenity

masters live by laws
of their making or choosing
they are free spirits
and have in their souls
what the Greeks call *kefi*
—a boundless joy
it is futile to try to explain
to lutherans and baptists

slaves are hatched every day
for restless and insignificant activity
all their exertions and mean appetites
merely fill up the vacuum of their lives

make yourselves invulnerable
to their stupidity
and their ill-will born of unsuccess
and resolve, my unseen darlings, to kill
any who would possess you
by convention or recreant twaddle
to kill without pity and remorse
and you can not be trapped or chained

HIT PARADE

Rejoicing in his body
he laughed and sang
but no one heard him

For in that land
the sickest was king
only laments would anyone sing

Only moanings
and sad songs of defeat
the whimpers of mutual comforting

Threnodies
and madrigals of unsuccess
dirges drear and slow

And brassy hymns
with which weakness cheers itself
and woman's eternal woe

THOUGHTS OF A MALE CHAUVINIST PIG

If you did not have
such *kefi* breasts
and admiral blue eyes
made for the open seas
and a tanned athlete's body
that each time you bend it
I see an archer's bow
about to let fly
its prize-winning shaft
who would be interested
in your journey
towards spiritual perfection
or your pitiful twaddle
about St. Thomas à Kempis?

THE SOLITARY

When I am heated up
with wine and incredible visions

And feel all-powerful,
my astral body striding over
hills and valleys
to plant itself like eidelweiss
on a lonely inaccessible mountain-top

When I am eloquent
with thoughts so subtle, so extraordinary
no poet before me
could ever conceive or utter them

When I know for certain
I could reach out and pluck the stars
one by one
and put them all into my notebook

Or that the moon and sun
shine only for my praise and celebration

And that the laughing gods love me
for my waywardness, priapic itch, imagination,
pride and the inextinguishable love
that warms me like a bonfire

And that I have only
to put out my hands
for them to close on history and luck
with the beautiful egotism
of blossoms and flies

I don't want you around me

THE ANIMAL ACROSS THE STREET

the animal across the street
makes himself comfortable
scratches his balls opens a can
of beer lights a cigarette
his window mine facing it
look down on the backside
of Amsterdam
in whose ulcerous cleft are
prostitutes fairies pimps pornshops
with blowups of haired cunt
that invite the world to drop in
                              stark naked
he picks up the cat
rubs its fur and shouts
endearments at it
in a tongue neither
I nor the cat understands
becomes enraged when the cat
curves from his onslaught of love
and commences to tease
then torture it till it screams
in his hands in disgust finally
flinging it hard against the wall
where it drops to the floor out of sight
he aims his erection
at the night from the centre of the room
and pathetically thin his long hair
falling in black matted curls
around his neck and shoulders
stands like a lonely apostle
supplicating conversion or alms

ANALOGUE

Alone on the seashore,
the soft dark wavelets
whispering at her feet,
the sexy romantic teenager
from Stockholm
(her father is a diplomat)
is looking at the coppercoloured moon
and sighing.

I stare fixedly
at the tight heartshaped ass
in the white jeans
(two perfect halfmoons)
and do the same.

HONEYMOON

She knocked his ribs, waking him.
'There's a hard object in bed,' she said.

He grumbled into her ear
it wasn't his erection
since he'd been fast asleep
and began to fumble between the sheets
thinking it might be lizard or beetle
when his fingers closed on her gold watch.

He held it from her, menacing her
with the unknown thing in the room's pitch
darkness
                'O Adam, O, O'

Such lovely birdcries from his little sparrow
such lovely birdcries. Yet half of him
stayed vengeful and sullen
for being awaked to ease his young wife's terror
and not for their bodies' swift embrace and pleasure.

FOR A YOUNG POET WHO HANGED HIMSELF

They're going, one by one they're going,
the bright, the original, the witty;
in their stead come
the acceptable sickies of our time

Sophists and conmen have built
a brothel on Mount Parnassus
where for popular wit
corpse dances with faggot

Benign and brainless
come the bearded gurus;
town-criers and demagogues
and women with woes

Wide open are the doors
wide, wide is the road;
joyless pedantic bores
head the parade

You saw the twisted footprints
walking one after the other
and as carefully as you selected a rhyme
you chose the hour of your departure

LURES

A wife's detestation
of her husband
after ten years of marriage
is equalled only
by that of a mother
for her burgeoning
attractive daughter

Servility
and repressed lasciviousness
affect the one; self-
lacerating jealousy
the other

The eternal feminine
lures to perfection
sang out the Olympian
to the mortals far below
as he sailed cleanly
over his seventh bar

FUNERARIA 'OLEA'

In bold black letters:
SERVICIO DIA Y NOCHE
Obviously this is not a dead business.

It is a thriving business.
Go in,
See for yourselves the white coffins
Lying in wait for the townspeople.

The tiniest caskets
Are the most numerous;
The women in these parts
Are always pregnant with them.

Zihuatanejo, Mexico

MEXICAN GUERRILLAS

Guerrillas with an ideology?

Bearded boobs
like Che
with a hole in his head
to let the sap run out?

You must be kidding.

These shoot
for the best reason in the world
—loot.

PORTRAIT OF SOMEONE I KNOW TOO WELL

Because he's not happy he always wants to instruct me:
one day it's how nations are governed
and what can be done to remove poverty and injustice;
another time his subject is fruit-bearing trees
and the good jellies that might be made of quince;
if I let him, he will lecture me endlessly
on the hexameters of Homer and Hesiod,
blazing out at the fools that mistake their use

I observe he's always angry about something:
clearly he wasn't consulted when the universe was made.
I think that's the one reason for his skepticism,
sheer vanity, though he'll laugh scornfully at my notion
and declare he never saw God wipe his ass
—if he did he'd believe and go to church;
he's of course lying and making bad theology
his ponderous alibi to be invidious and crude

Whatever he feels at the time becomes a standard;
if he's unwell and morose then it's certainly pessimism
everyone must at once embrace, even the cheerful corncrakes;
when he's exuberant because he's been lucky at cards
or with a woman no one is more supermanic,
no one can quote Nietzsche with more assured effect.
Rustic, sophisticate, vulgarian, scholar, wit
he turns them around as a fine chef does his spit

No doubt he possesses a mine of information
and throws his heavy ingots at everyone's head:
put it all down to an unslaked hunger for greatness.
I'd have him gaze quietly at that tiny island
unmoving in the haze like the fin of a dozing shark,
at the colours of those clouds those hills those ancient roofs
and feel on his naked skin the warmed-up sun
hauling him gently heavenward limb by limb

A TAILOR'S VIEW OF HISTORY

Marx was mistaken:
It's the runts
Who make history

Never the masses.
Thread and needle
In hand I think

Of Napoleon and Caesar
And this century's
Four Horsemen

Of the Apocalypse
Two of whom would've looked better
Wearing toupees

Miserable shorties
Whose vaulting ambition
Was to strut on a pile of corpses

So they could spit
On the skulls
Of men taller than themselves

While Joe Blow
Wiping his wet eyelids
Looked up and hurrahed.

Some historians
Call it
Grandeur

ADAM AND EVE

By turns poet
and Dionysian philosopher
he speaks of deep dark things

With passion he speaks
(as always)
and with thrilling eloquence
about life and death
about poetry
about hatred and evil
gods and children

Enthralled, she feels
her clitoris
begin to itch
and her vagina
grow moist
with soft explosions
of desire

REVOLUTION

He has a black tuft of hair
under his capacious chin
and not a wisp on his head

'Lord, turn my face upsidedown'
is each night's quiet prayer
when he trundles off to bed

MARRIAGE

The lover of the treacherous wife
dribbled poison into the king's ear

In no time the fair regal body
that had known only perfumes and oils

Blossomed with hideous pustules;
boils covered it from crown to toe

Ugly under the sun, the sleeping king
gave up his ghost to the battlements

One dark night a poet saw the powerless shade
and gave to it an immortal voice

PEACOCK

Moving slow and gorgeous
as in the feathered radiance
of a dream
and without defence
as Beauty and Delight
always have been,
he's the poet among birds

Only in a cage
where he can strut and astound
is he secure
from claws and fangs
indifferent
to the elegant loveliness
of his elongated vulnerable tail

Pride-besotted creature
to have so many eyes
and to be so blind

SOME OTHER DAY

In the morning I smoked my cigarette
had a cup of black coffee
and carefully went over my plan
for the destruction of the world

At night I rejoiced
alone in my room
at having put aside my scheme
to annihilate the world and all its inhabitants,
discovering once again
that great events roar over mankind
like the sea over the inert
stones and pebbles on the beach
and hearing the Greek fruit peddlers
shout through the narrow streets of Mithymna:
'Orea pragmata! Orea pragmata!
Beautiful things. I have beautiful things to sell.'

But it was the black kitten
I saw rolled up in the sunshine
like a tiny ball of fur
that stopped my thoughts like a period

THE BLACK QUEEN

Having the face of a worldlywise Greek cat
he tells me how one late afternoon
he was sleeping on the white sand
with a scorpion only inches from his head
readying its black stub
                      when his wife
who saw the menace from where she stood
awakened him with a harsh whisper
so this thing of death would not strike
from shock or sudden fear
                      and as if
the innocent shingle were a launching pad
he sprang up from his rosy dreams of life
and with a stone roiled the foul blackness
into the sand like the devil's instep

I tell him how I once swam solitary
through a minefield of jellyfish
and got myself stung in the eye
                      I saw
huge blue and yellow stars light up the water
and dance till they disappeared among the ferns
but the bright blister on my face was a reflex
I saw the green world through for weeks afterwards
and the mist
            on either side of the wide horizon

After that we played cards
and I pulled a straight flush
                      queen spade high

MITHYMNA CEMETERY

The villagers use it merely to pull off the flesh
from the skeleton,
then they come for the bones if they're not bones themselves
and bury them in the back yard

This busy traffic has gone on for centuries:
year in year out
corpses in skeletons out,
the bones cleaner
than the wings of that butterfly
hovering over my feet

The whitewashed walls are almost as tall as the cypresses
to keep the dead from clambering over them;
when the aging sexton closes the gate
you know they are all locked in securely for the night

Behind it the blue waters wrinkle and spume

The barren treeless hills
have not changed their places in aeons

Alcaeus and Sappho
may have sat on the selfsame stone
I am sitting on now
and looked out at them and at the sea

I should like to think so
it makes death's victory somehow less complete

THE BASIN

A plastic basin
pale-blue, pale-green:
completely out of her depths
and at sea
among the savage rocks;
pushed here, tossed rudely there
she rides everything
with superb self-assurance
and takes each rebuff
as though meant for someone else;
knowing victory
lies in unending patience
for when entirely
filled to the brim
Neptune himself must swallow
his pride
and take her in.

MOLIBOS CAT

Her eyes are round with suspicion.
At your approach she runs away.
Children and grown-ups are her enemy,
not dogs which she can lick in a fair fight

Dogs don't suddenly kick a pregnant cat
for no reason at all
or blind her with a pointed stick.
No dog ever poured naphthalene on her fur
and afterwards put a lighted match to her tail.
No dog ever wanted to hobble her for life
by sawing off one of her front paws

She has been around humans for a long time
and knows their true nature
—knows it better than Blaise Pascal
who flopped down on his knees and prayed.
Look at her curled up on the ledge;
even in sleep her long face is reserved and melancholy.

One can imagine Heraclitos, the weeping philosopher,
looking like that

AFTERNOON OF A DYING SATYR

Two things
revived
the dying satyr

The Greek sun
and woman's amorality

And the third:
a plane crash

Now he takes nothing
seriously

Not even truth
and certainly not
death

ARCHILOCHUS CURSES THE WOMAN WHO JILTED HIM

Your tits, may they grow red and tight as boils
And be without cure from healing serums
That when you hold your babe to give him suck
They spurt thick pus between his toothless gums.

MADONNA AND DIONYSOS

Over Dionysos
the sly madonna
softly lets fall her halo
like a hollowed circular blade:
she sighs, hearing the desired sound,
and lifts her eyes to heaven

How beatifically she smiles
when he presents his snipped balls to her
as lilies-of-the-valley in full bloom
and pomegranates
that bleed into her palm
or as clouds of lofty sentiment
smelling of incense

How serene and sweet
is the smile on the face
of that white spider

My son, knock all her teeth out
and present them gallantly,
one by one,
to the votarist of her choosing

THE IDEAL AMONG VACATIONISTS

I pick myself up from the beach
to leave my impress on the stones and pebbles

Visible to no one else but me,
it is intact and infrangible as a concept

It is also more permanent than caves or mountains:
not even the tide can haul it into the sea

Each time I look for it, it is plainly there
like Honoré de Balzac's covert masterpiece

Sunbathers trip over it, mistakenly thinking
it is a stone bigger and more jagged than the rest

Who knows how many other outlines lie beside it
and whether Eternity has made them restless

Like them it too is cold to middle-class Athenians
whose churning mouths spit out clichés and *tzatziki*

However fiery, the sun cannot use my figure
to fry the oils and creams dripping from their bodies

It is indifferent to dowries and gold watches
for in the dark the constellations keep guard over it

When I return early next morning
I shall see my ideal shape sprouting between the stones

MUSEUM AT IRAKLION

A place
where ugly people
come to look
at beautiful things

And where
in polychromed sarcophagi
the fleshless skulls
still wrapt
in their Minoan dreams
seem more vital
in their quiet
off-hand way
than the grey faces
of the 20th-century homunculi
come to stare at them

PROTEUS AND NYMPH

For Molly

I put down my book
    and stare at the distant haze;
the loud-voiced Greeks around me
    chomping on their fish and *peponi*
must reckon I'm having age-old thoughts
    on the human condition.
Noisy fools. I'm thinking of the waves
    gently cupping the breasts
of the lovely nymph just risen from the sea
    and the water lapping
her thighs and her delicate love-cleft

When she swims away
    she pulls my thoughts after her
in watery streaks of light. I become
    the sea around her
and she nestles in my long green arms
    or is held in the flowing
wavelets of my white hair. I billow
    above her like a dolphin
stroke her limbs and nip her rosy neck and shoulders
    with sharp unceasing kisses
till languorously she slips to the ribbed sand
    where under the haloing starfish
fern weed and enamoured seasnake I quiver
    between her silver thighs

AMERICAN YOUNG WOMAN IN PATMOS

an x-ray of her skull
will reveal a sponge
it has the shape and outline
of the human brain
but don't be fooled
it's a sponge alright

it delights to mop up everything in sight

bile pondscum monks' piss church smells
and cultured feculence of every kind
so long as it's absorbable
to its eager open large generous
American pores

occasionally and by pure chance
even fresh sparkling water

when it can't hold another drop
it feels heavy and satisfied
and sits down
to write a long letter
to Mom and Dad and Lucy Poo back home

GANYMEDE

Sitting in a taverna
among garrulous life-loving Greeks,
the morning sunshine
falling on tables and glasses,
I am suddenly pierced
by a Jove-sent arrow
of unreasonable joy

It was Ganymede
who nipped me with it,
a smiling rogue of six
gathering the bottletops
lying on the floor
like fallen miniature crowns
and emptying
their small bowls of sunlight
into his pockets

I greet him
with a secret sign
and my old eyes
are as gay as his

APOKALYPSIS

In the famed monastery
I watched the neat black-gowned monks
at their prayers and genuflections

Under the pagan sun
comfortable on its worn stones
I counted twelve ants
hauling a sacrificial fly
across my thumb:
they were tireless in their long devotions
and their shoulders were flecked with dust

*Monastery of St. John the Theologue,
Patmos*

GREEK FLY

Wings filled with divine inner chaos

Bringing bazouki music to chairs, walls, tables
and the long thin ouzo glasses on the table
or taking its inspired frenzies up to the ceiling,
spotted picture frames and oleographs
or to the taciturn wife and husband whose day
begins with their disappointment in each other

Rubbing the golden moments between its legs
the rapturous fly comes to rest on a nail
making it buzz with the unceasing malice
of an old woman's tongue: the kitchen
is loud with its dry bright-hued gossip and abuse;
then landing on my shoulder the fly announces
to saucepans, forks, still uneaten eggs
and to all the crumbs the splendid news
that my poems like my vaccinated arm
are good for all borders

Shifting to another fleshly promontory
it stands on one leg like a proud Talmudic scholar
and recites the entire Odyssey
and is about to begin the Iliad
when catching sight of itself in the mirror
it leaps into the air like Nureyev
and gives a breath-taking performance
of a fly chasing itself until it's caught

The fly brings ripe hayfields into the room
the smell of cows and summer barnyards
the innocence of children clapping their hands in play
Mao and the Chinese revolution that sent it here
and all the poems ever written about mortality
and Emily dying to its ever fainter buzz;
head between its legs it thinks hard about life's brevity
then like a mad Euripidean Greek it drops
a billion eggs to fertilize its unkillable tragic splendour

It takes chances, this fly, like a poet;
it threads the air under the wife's frown
and recklessly settles on her puckered forehead
as if it were the face of Papadopoulos lying in his coffin
then shamelessly cleans its legs before her eyes
when her loathing for her husband in her open palm
descends on it with all the unerring ferocity
of repressed lasciviousness and thirteen years
of successful marriage

There it lies on the floor
waiting for the funeral orations to begin

Molibos, Lesbos,
August 6, 1973

POET ON COS

for 'Mike' Varvarikos

living on a Greek island
and swimming each day
in the health-giving Aegean
and having all the sweet ass
a man his years can safely handle,
when the landlady's rooster wakes him
at dawn
his first thought is:
do people out there
still read those twilight rooks
Yeats and Eliot?
those two sexless frauds
Frost and Auden?

and the hens hopping like mad
before the spry rooster
cluck 'yah-k' 'yah-k' 'yah-k'

the world is sicker
than I supposed is his next thought
and goes back to sleep

GREEK EPIGRAM

For Peggy Sylvia

On air mattresses till dusk from earliest morn
They watch, inert as pebbles, the waves' ebb and flow.
'Lie-lows,' you called them, turning up your mouth in scorn,
You who reverenced the radiant god Apollo
Though your frame ill and by the god you loved forlorn.
Now, dear, quieter than they you lie, and more low.

MADMAN

Hindus
worship monkeys and cows

Muslims and Jews
an unseen remarkable god
who never did them any good

Christians,
a perforated corpse

Buddhists
speak in hushed tones of Nothing

The children of Han
revere the ideograms of Confucius

And the Japanese
genuflect to the bones of their dead
ancestors

He reverences only his body's self
and the joyful truths
that surface daily from it

JIJIMUGE

making poems
making love
I see both sides of the coin
with one perception
I become my son
my son becomes me
I and my son are one

master, let my silence
like the silence of beauty
describe their non-existence
with perfect candour

ASIAN SUITE

Jai Hind

Lakschmi
on a lotus leaf

Tilak
on a face of ineffable sadness

Ganga,
life-giving mother
to whom her children finally return
as bones and ash

Shiva-Vishnu,
destroyer and preserver
of lepers cows children sadhus milkshakes
dung

Kali,
radiant black goddess smiling
and fingering her necklace of skulls

Pompish Binny's
Art Gallery and Curio's Shop

Siam

I have seen
          the future

And it works

Alas

Frangapani petals floating on petrol

Bamboo Shoot

If I had women and wine
And all of China to roam
I'd find the ghost of Li Po
And match him poem for poem

Hong Kong

The gilded rectum of Asia

CONVERSION

She walks in deformity on all fours,
her belly sweeping
the filthy streets

In this city of burning ghats
where misery
scrapes the cadaver's rose embers
into a pan
to cook her evening meal
and gurus
expound wisdom and goodness
from a cowsplatter
deformities are as manifold
as the agitated butterflies
hovering over fosse and ditch
—each one more harrowing than the other

But the proud magnificent beasts
that shook once the green forests:
they are gone forever

Benares,
October 25, 1973

RAVENS

A luxury meal
at the Hotel de Paris
a soft belch
and afterwards for easing mint
under a juniper tree
—the hoarse croak
of ravens overhead—
any one of a score
of beliefs modern and ancient
to make you forget
the betel-red mouth
of the rickshaw man
waiting outside the gates,
his dead eyes smouldering
like charcoal

CH'AN ARTIST

Through the loving contemplation
of transiency and mutability
I received a foretaste of eternity
and saw with luminous certitude
that the wheel turned and did not turn

Drawing a roseleaf for ten years
I flowed at last into the leaf;
I shuddered at the raindrop's touch
till I became raindrop and splash:
now I draw the roseleaf perfectly

YOUNG COUPLE AT LUM FONG HOTEL

When I see you
              smiling
at each other
and nakedly showing
the appetite in your hands and eyes

I forget the chattering old men
              with bladder trouble
and slack-bellied blear-eyed women
who moan
              over their hard nocturnal stools
as once with equal vehemence
they rocked and moaned
in the furious exertions of love

Each other's unbreaking pole
              of imagination and love
you vault over
              wisdom greying at the roots
and smelling of unalterable defeats,
the will-to-power that fleers
              out of skincreases and hemorrhoids

O my oblivious lovers
from my table
              I applaud silently
as you rise
with perfect grace and disdain

Penang,
December 7, 1973

BODHIDHARMA

From what sputtering taper
was my light kindled
... to sputter in its turn?

Detached iotas of flame
fall into the Vast Emptiness
to turn up fragments of poems
floating on its nearest facet.
I roar with furious laughter.

My pleasure in discomfiting
enemies and friends alike
is a gift from the Gautama himself.

And wherever I turn
I meet myself
striding the other way.

At sudden moments
power can come flooding in
from unseen major stars, from geese
and leaping goats
to soak all my follicles
in the sweetness of Buddhi.

That's why my face
looks like a clenched fist
and I am always irascible.

THE THREE SISTERS

Out of the haze of blue greenness,
the high valley's clear immense silence
rise up these Noachian giantesses

On either side of the bald absurd one
stand her rough rockhewn sisters,
each topped with a blur of trees

From the metal railing a man sees
the on-camera lice moving slowly
under their close-cropped green hair

Katoomba, N.S.W.

AUSTRALIAN BUSH

I am about to get lost
in the Australian bush

Behind me
dusty and obscure
stretches the road convicts
laid down
        their lives for;
in front the ghostly gumtrees
drop their skins
like snakes

The bush is a wily old grandmother
that never had children,
forever wiping the grey-green ichor
streaming from her eyes

Birdcries are lost in her hair
and become one more smudge

I am startled
by the dry silence
into which my flesh sinks
as if I were a swaddled whisper,
by the low-breathing absence
that takes me quietly in

All the brown dead leaves
strewn along the road
keep telling me
        there's no death,
the black wounds and sores
of dateless trunks
              mouth my resurrection

Why then does the knowing
not refresh or gladden

Why instead
do I sit down at the sanded rim
feeling suddenly burdened and weary
as if the agonized trees
had lowered
              all their accumulated aeons
onto my fragile human back

ENCOUNTER WITH A REPTILE

I was sitting on a rock
writing a poem
when a black snake
uncoiled before me.

It was long and sleek
and looked poisonous.

'Look,' I said to it,
'you don't scare me the least bit.
I've met more venomous snakes
than you
in Sydney. So get lost.'

The wounded reptile
gave a sudden shudder or two
then picked itself
huffily
off the ground
and started to walk
towards Bathurst.

THE COASTAL MIND

On the electric train
that's taking me to Gosford
what I think of
                as it rounds
the long solitary beaches and lagoons
is how Wagner
                      would be out of place here
too melodramatic too noisy too showing off
Bach, yes, maybe Sibelius or Mahler
Mendelssohn and Bizet definitely not
                                  Yet
ultimately this country will make
its own music
                uneuropean
as its marsupials
and like them wary
of softer more tender responses

From
      the rattling little train
separating me from the sunshine and gloom
of Sydney the beerdrinking nihilists
who meet each Friday at the same pub
houses sheds petrol stations bridges
drop into the dry white mouth of space
forever open to gulp
                          and excrete them
unchewed yet crumbling visibly
at the foot
of the impenetrable bush

                     Everything human
in this huge dead continent is pushed
to that green periphery: the painted gates cars
children tools and red bulldozers
I see with turned head
                          now leaking softly
into the diminishing distance
even the coastal mind running after them
that contemplates   holds on   finally lets go

POLE-VAULTER

Now that grey fluff
covers my chest
and it's the glasses on my nose
that sparkle, not my eyes
what the horny girls
                want from me
is advice on
how to allure young men;
                        those
with ideas in their head
and pimples on their ass,
my final opinion
on the Theaetetus

They say at my age
I should be guru or sage,
not foolishly behave
like passion's slave

Ignorant trulls
in a cold land;
age will dry their flesh
and wrinkle it with useless folds.
Spry and drugged with love
I pole-vault
                over my grave

ACKNOWLEDGEMENTS

For permission to reprint I owe grateful thanks to the editors of the following publications in which several poems in the present volume first appeared:

The Canadian Forum
Counter/Measures
The Unmuzzled Ox
Ariel
Saturday Night
New
Canadian Literature
Chronicle Review
The Toronto Star
Manna
Anvil Blood
Dialog
The Australian
Rufus

I also wish to thank the Canada Council for an Award which allowed me to travel to Europe, Southeast Asia, the moon and several of the lesser known stars, thereby replenishing my stock of metaphors and providing me so many experiences it will take another Award to enable me to puzzle out what they mean.